D0552061

speaking and listening in multilingual classrooms

Viv Edwards

YORK ST. JOHN
COLLEGE LIBRARY

WITHDRAWN

2 0 APR 2022

Reading and Language Information Centre
University of Reading

York St. John College

3 8025 00475567 7

To Redlands Primary School, for 14 years of rich experience

Acknowledgments

Grateful thanks to Angela Redfern and Prue Goodwin for reading and commenting on various drafts; and to the staff, children and parents at Redlands Primary School and Prospect School, Reading, for allowing us to take photographs.

Meeting the needs of bilingual pupils

This book is part of a series of training materials which consists of three separate packs:

- *Reading in multilingual classrooms*
- *Writing in multilingual classrooms*
- *Speaking and listening in multilingual classrooms*

Each pack comprises:

- a course leader's handbook
- overhead transparencies
- handouts
- a teacher's book

The teacher's books are also available separately.

Publications of related interest

Other titles from the Reading and Language Information Centre of interest to teachers in multilingual classrooms include:

Building bridges: multilingual resources for children
Multilingual Resources for Children Project

The AIMER Year Book
Annually updated lists of anti-racist, multicultural teaching materials to support all areas of the curriculum, as well as community language teaching and language support teaching.

The multicultural guide to children's literature 0 – 12
Edited by Rosemary Stones

Working with parents
Penny Kenway

© Viv Edwards 1995
ISBN 0 7049 07801

Reading and Language Information Centre
University of Reading
Bulmershe Court
Earley
Reading RG6 1HY

Contents

Introduction

Attitudes towards the spoken language have undergone dramatic changes. The realization that talk plays a vital role in learning, and that children are active participants in this process, has led to fundamental changes in classroom organization. The realization that all language skills – speaking and listening, reading and writing – are interrelated, each making a contribution to progress in the others, has also influenced the kinds of activities offered to children.

The presence in many classrooms of second language learners is another development which has helped to focus teachers' minds on the optimal conditions for learning. Multilingual classrooms are now common in cities throughout the English speaking world and in many European countries. In some locations, the majority of children will come from one speech community; in others, there is a dazzling array of different languages.

In the early days, new arrivals were usually taught in segregated classes by specialist language teachers. Over time, it has become clear that the mainstream classroom potentially offers a richer learning environment. Yet class and subject teachers have often been required to take increasing responsibility for language learners with little or no training.

This book explores the many aspects of speaking and listening in multilingual classrooms. In particular, it looks at:

- the central role of talk in the learning process
- issues relating to linguistic diversity which have implications for equal opportunities
- what teachers need to know about the background and the learning needs of bilingual children
- what teachers need to do to support bilingual children's learning
- ways of using linguistic diversity as a classroom resource
- the assessment of speaking and listening.

Talking to learn

Ideas about the role of talk in learning have undergone a quiet revolution. Very few people now believe that children should be seen not heard, or that they should only speak when they are spoken to. Schools have changed, too, and many teachers would be horrified at the suggestion that, when children are talking, they are simply wasting time.

Of course, talk has always been important in school, but for many years it was the teacher's talk that counted, not the children's. Our understanding of how people learn has become a great deal more sophisticated over the years. The Swiss psychologist, Jean Piaget, was the first to challenge traditional thinking. His research led him to believe that children are active learners, not passive observers. The teacher's job was to encourage them to make their own discoveries by moving objects, counting them, putting them together and so on. This view of learning was influential from the 1960s onwards.

Piaget's idea of children as active learners was an important piece in a complex puzzle. The Russian psychologist Vygotsky (1978) has also had a profound effect on educational thinking. His particular contribution was to stress the social nature of learning in which speaking and listening play a vital role.

The work of Jerome Bruner (eg 1986) draws extensively on Vygotsky. He, too, attaches great importance to the centrality of talk in the development of knowledge and understanding, a view which has achieved increasing support since the 1980s.

Talk in the classroom

When researchers started looking critically at classroom talk, they weren't always very happy with what they found (Wood *et al* 1980). On the one hand, teachers were usually good at establishing rapport with children. When little William announced, 'I'm going to play with cars,' he could expect an enthusiastic response of, 'Oh lovely!' or something similar. On the other hand, they spent a lot of time using 'management talk' to organize the children – 'Charlotte, I think you'd better wipe your nose. Can you go and find a tissue?' – and, all too often, they failed to make more intellectual demands of children.

Teachers tended to dominate in classrooms: they asked questions of a testing nature and they didn't give children enough chance to think and answer. It seems that children talk in greater depth and at greater length to adults who offer their own personal views instead of bombarding them with questions.

The situation with older children was scarcely more encouraging. Here the main model was of 'talk and chalk' with the teacher assuming control of a rather narrow range of question and answer routines. Even in whole class discussion, children had relatively little opportunity to make a contribution. According to one calculation, if all of class time were spent in discussion and this time evenly divided, each child would be entitled to ten minutes talk a week!

One alternative to pupil-teacher talk is talk within small groups. The peer group provides a supportive environment where children are able to explore and take risks. By putting ideas into their own words, children make them their own. They also need the opportunity to use talk in more formal situations, such as reporting the findings of their own group to the whole class, or making a presentation in assembly. The experience gained in small group work makes formal talk much less daunting.

All classroom talk needs very careful planning to achieve the best results (Open University 1991). In 1987 a major project, the National Oracy Project, set out to sensitize teachers as to how they could encourage more effective talk. A number of basic findings emerged from their work:

- By explaining an idea, we come to understand it more clearly.

- Active listening helps us to understand the ideas, knowledge and feelings of other people.

- When children talk among themselves, they can explore concepts, try out theories, express opinions and get immediate feedback.

- Dialogue between a child and a more skilled person is a very powerful way to learn.

- When teachers observe children's talk they learn a great deal about what children know and how they think.

In the view of talk embedded in these findings, the teacher's job is to provide 'scaffolding' for children's learning. Just as the scaffolding is taken down when a building is finished, the good teacher is someone who allows children to take over control for their own learning. This works best:

- when teachers use what children say and do to plan activities that move them on

- when children understand why they're being asked to take part in a particular activity

- by judging how and when to intervene so that children can make sense of their discoveries and failures

- by deciding when to withdraw so that children can be responsible for their own learning.

Teachers have been slow to translate research evidence into practice and many schools still rely heavily on traditional methods. All the same, new understandings of the critical role which talk plays in the learning process have had a considerable impact on classroom organization and the kinds of activities which children are offered.

Every child's entitlement

Language is is an essential tool for learning. It is also inextricably linked with who we are and can trigger powerful social, gender and racial stereotypes. If children are to fulfil their educational potential, teachers need to look very carefully at their attitudes towards different languages and how these may favour some groups over others.

Standard and non-standard English

There is a long history of negative attitudes towards different languages and dialects. The 1921 Newbolt Report on *The Teaching of English in England*, for instance, made it quite clear that:

> It is definitely the business of the elementary school to teach all its pupils who either speak a definite dialect or whose speech is disfigured by vulgarisms, to speak standard English, and to speak it clearly and with expression.

Similar opinions are still expressed today, with many advocates of standard English taking the moral high ground. Norman Tebbit used a Radio 4 broadcast as a platform for his views on this subject:

> We've allowed so many standards to slip ... teachers weren't properly bothering to teach kids to spell and punctuate properly ... if you allow standards to slip to the stage where good English is no better than bad English, where people turn up filthy ... at school ... all those things cause people to have no standards at all, and once you lose standards then there is no imperative to stay out of crime. (Cited in Graddol & Swann, 1988)

Attitudes towards some overseas varieties of English have been equally unenlightened. The Association of Teachers of Pupils from Overseas (1970), for instance, described the language of West Indian children as 'babyish,' 'careless and slovenly' and 'very relaxed like the way they walk.' The National Association of School Masters (1969), for their part, advised members that Caribbean children spoke 'a kind of plantation English which is socially unacceptable and inadequate for communication.'

Language deprivation?

> ... For some time, the work of Basil Bernstein (1973) added a veneer of academic respectability to prejudices about the inadequacy of non-standard English. He put forward the idea of two language codes – the elaborated and the restricted – which differed in grammar and vocabulary. The restricted code was seen as exploiting fewer linguistic resources and dependent on shared meanings. The elaborated code, in contrast, allowed the speaker to express meaning explicitly and was not context bound.

Bernstein argued that different patterns of socialization were responsible for the different distribution of the codes, and seemed to be equating the restricted code with working class and the elaborated code with middle class speakers. It is easy to understand the appeal of this theory, since it provides a possible explanation for why some children do better than others at school. Children who don't have access to the elaborated code will be at a disadvantage in an educational system concerned with making meaning explicit through language.

However, Bernstein's views have been severely criticized. For instance, he shows little awareness how children change their speech according to situation. William Labov (1973), in contrast, shows that social setting can transform a child who may appear 'non-verbal' or 'monosyllabic' into an effective communicator. In an interview at school, Leon, an eight year old African-American child, at first gives short, non-committal answers to the questions put to him. Later, his best friend is invited to join him, everyone (including the interviewer) sits on the floor, food is passed around and taboo subjects are introduced into the conversation. The social distance between adult and child is reduced and Leon behaves like a normal eight year old who speaks fluently and intelligently.

Labov also makes another important observation: qualities such as logic are more properly associated with the speaker than the language that they use. Middle class speakers of standard English often offer inconsistent arguments. By the same token, working class non-standard speakers are capable of arguing persuasively and with logical consistency.

Although notions of language deprivation have been discredited, teachers are often held to be the experts on how parents should speak to their children. Sometimes they make assumptions about what parents do which fail to stand up to close examination. It is still widely believed, for instance, that some parents – and particularly those from working class backgrounds – don't speak to their children either often enough or in the right way. Health visitors have been told to urge parents to 'bathe their children in language'. In one project in Birmingham in the 1980s, health visitors, speech therapists and social workers made contact with inner city mothers in supermarkets and even gave out 'Mum, talk to me' stickers to children (Edwards 1983).

We know now that this concern was completely misplaced. In particular, the work of Barbara Tizard & Martin Hughes (1984) has made it clear that the differences between the language used by working class and middle class families are very small. Ironically, the main differences are between home and school. At home, conversations are usually longer and there is a better balance between adult and child. Children ask more questions and adults answer them more often. There is every reason to believe that parents intuitively do a good job of developing their children's language. The ratio of adults to children in the home makes it much easier to give individual attention and to pursue questions in depth.

Bilingualism

The same negative attitudes which have been documented for non-standard dialects of English also apply to other languages. Bilingualism has a history of bad press. It is still widely assumed that the brain has only a finite capacity, so that bilingual children learn neither of their languages as well as monolingual children. A large number of studies undertaken in Britain and North America up to the 1960s supported this view (see, for instance, Peal & Lambert 1962), arguing that bilingualism is an intellectual handicap and that children should be encouraged to forget their first languages as rapidly as possible.

However, these studies have serious methodological flaws. Sometimes they compared middle class monolinguals with working class bilinguals from schools in poor neighbourhoods; sometimes they failed to take into account that one language is nearly always more dominant than the other and tested children in their weaker language.

It has also been suggested that bilingualism is a serious emotional handicap. The Department of Education and Science (1971), for instance, described the 'bilingual situation' as 'very bewildering' and potentially giving rise to 'psychological and emotional insecurity.'

Although such negative views are now much less common, there are still reports of children who are asked not to 'jabber in Gujarati' in the playground, or to pay a penny fine each time they are heard speaking their home language in class. Sharan, a nine year old year old Bangladeshi child, describes her own experience thus:

> Sometimes like we are talking in the playground and someone English comes along then like we kind of stop and start talking English 'cos I think I'm going to get the mick taken out of me … Some of them don't even know what we're talking about then they go and tell the teacher and some of the teachers will say don't talk in your own language because other people can't understand it … And the children say to you there is no place for Indians in this school and country and things. They say go back to your own country so that people can understand you. (Savva 1990: 250, 252)

An alternative point of view

Negative views of bilingualism have been challenged in recent years on several different fronts. We now understand that speaking two or more languages does not create unnecessary strain. Despite surface differences, various cognitive and academic skills such as literacy are transferable from one language to another; they don't have to be relearned.

A child's ability to transfer skills, however, would appear to depend on their competence in the first language. Jim Cummins (1984) proposes that children's level of competence in the second language is related, in part at least, to the level of competence they have developed in the first language when intensive exposure to the second language begins. Children with a solid foundation in the first language will be able to transfer skills from one language to another without further teaching.

It has also been pointed out that there is a history of double standards in this area: bilingualism is considered a handicap only for less powerful members of society. Bilingualism has not proved to be a problem for children from English speaking homes attending either Welsh schools or French immersion programs in Canada. The critical difference between French-English and Welsh-English bilinguals, on the one hand, and Bengali-English or Panjabi-English bilinguals, on the other is that, in one case, the children learning a second language belong to a high status group and, in the other, they come from a low status group.

There is now widespread recognition of the social and personal benefits of bilingualism: a sound foundation in the language(s) of the home increases children's self-esteem and confidence in their own ethnicity; it is important for good relations within the family; and it increases the range of vocational options open to children.

In a school environment where linguistic diversity is promoted as an asset rather than a problem, there are benefits for both monolinguals and bilinguals. Such an approach increases monolingual children's knowledge about language; it also raises the status of bilingual children. It can contribute to combating racism by raising awareness of cultural diversity and improving communication between different cultural groups.

Running through the arguments about the benefits of bilingualism is the assumption that racial equality in education demands a positive response to linguistic diversity. Teachers should build on the skills and knowledge that children bring with them to school. Children will feel more confident and secure when their languages are valued and respected than when they are ignored or treated with contempt. Acceptance of linguistic diversity is an essential feature of all good educational practice.

Stereotypes

So why have negative views of linguistic diversity been so persistent? Our attitudes to language are so deeply entrenched that we try to rationalize our likes and dislikes. Many people have a gut feeling, for instance, that some accents and dialects are intrinsically more beautiful than others. Two competing hypotheses have been proposed to explain this conviction: the 'inherent value' hypothesis holds that there is something intrinsic to certain accents which makes them more pleasant; the 'imposed norm' hypothesis proposes that the accepted pleasantness of certain varieties simply reflects the high status of their speakers.

It is possible to test these hypotheses by using 'judges' unfamiliar with the language or dialect in question: if high status can be explained in terms of some intrinsic quality, the judges will comes to the same conclusions as native speakers. Greek speakers, for instance, are unanimous that the Athenian dialect has highest status and that Cretan speech sounds unsophisticated. However, English speaking judges are divided between those who prefer Cretan, those who like Athenian and those who simply cannot make a choice. Experiments of this kind thus suggest that there is nothing inherent in certain languages and dialects which makes them more attractive than others. Rather we are influenced by social stereotypes.

The educational implications of linguistic stereotypes

Our speech tells people as much about us as the clothes we wear or where we live. It gives clues about where we come from, our ethnic background and our social class. But it can also act as a trigger for stereotypes which bear no relationship to truth. This tendency has serious implications for educational outcomes. If children are considered less favourably because of the way that they speak, low teacher expectations may well prove to be self-fulfiling prophecies.

There are strong indications that these concerns are well-founded. A consistent pattern of responses emerges from experiments using many different language varieties, including French, English, Greek, Jewish and African American English (Edwards 1989). In all cases, judges listened to recorded speech, unaware that one of the speakers is heard twice – once using the high status variety, the second time the low status variety. In every case, speakers of the high status dialect or language are considered more intelligent and competent.

In a British context, a similar pattern of responses emerged in an experiment with student teachers who judged recordings of a middle class White boy, a working class White girl, a recently arrived Jamaican girl and a British born Barbadian girl who spoke twice – once using a working class English accent and once a Barbadian dialect (Edwards 1979). The middle class boy was consistently evaluated most favourably: he was felt to be more intelligent, better behaved and so on. Next came the two working class recordings, one White, the other Black, followed by the two Caribbean children. The point of greatest importance here is that the same child was judged more positively in her English than in her Caribbean 'guise'. The student teachers were also prepared to make judgements about the children's educational outcomes, predicting high academic success for the middle class boy and very low levels of achievement for the Black children.

The findings of this research need to be interpreted with caution. The judges were students and not practising teachers. They were placed in a very artificial situation and there can be no certainty that they would be influenced by the stereotypes in real life. But, at the very least, this pattern of reactions should alert us to the danger that stereotypes may lead to low teacher expectations of various groups of children which may, in turn, result in educational underperformance.

What teachers need to know

Teachers need to understand the nature of linguistic stereotyping and how this can adversely affect the educational outcomes of non-standard English speaking children. They also need to be informed about the backgrounds and the educational needs of the children that they teach. It is important to appreciate, for instance, that bilingual children are not a homogeneous group. It is a basic courtesy to find out as much as possible about their languages, religions and naming practices. Teachers also have a responsibility to identify and respond appropriately to cultural differences in communication. Equally important, they need a basic understanding of the language learning process.

The extent of diversity

Bilingual children are a very disparate group. Some, like the Panjabi Sikhs and Moslems, belong to communities established in Britain since the 1950s; others like the Somalis, the Tamils and the Bosnians are more recent arrivals, fleeing from political turmoil in their home countries. Even within the same linguistic community, there may be important differences. Panjabi speakers who arrived in Britain via East Africa tend to come from middle class homes and have a high level of education; Panjabi speakers who arrived directly from India and Pakistan tend to come from rural backgrounds and may have had little formal education.

In many inner city areas, the majority of the school population speak one or more languages in addition to English. In some of these schools, many students come from one linguistic minority community; in others, thirty or more different languages may be spoken. In contrast, bilingual children in more outlying areas may find themselves attending predominantly monoethnic, monolingual schools.

Children from minority language backgrounds also vary in their linguistic preferences. It would be wrong to assume, for instance, that children speak English as a second language simply because they come from a linguistic minority community: many families make a decision to use English as the language of the home. Nor can we assume that children will necessarily want to develop the language of their parents and grandparents.

All the same, there is a substantial body of evidence which shows that languages in addition to English are widely used in many ethnic minority homes. It is also a matter of record that very large numbers of families from many different speech communities send their children to classes in community or heritage languages both inside and outside mainstream schools (Alladina & Edwards 1991; Cummins & Danesi 1990).

Who speaks what?

A number of terms including 'mother tongues', 'first languages' and 'home languages' have been used over the years to describe the languages spoken in minority communities. The terminological confusion mirrors the complex linguistic reality. Italian, for instance, cannot be described as the first or home language of third generation Italians who have always spoken English but go to special classes to learn the language of their parents and grandparents. Moslem children who speak Panjabi in the family may attend classes in Urdu, the language of religion and 'high culture.' Nor can a language studied in a formal setting of this kind be described as a 'mother tongue'. The use of 'community languages' in Britain and Australia and 'heritage languages' in Canada avoids many of these pitfalls by moving the focus from the individual to the wider community.

Children often say that they speak 'Indian' or 'Pakistani' or 'African' rather than Gujarati or Panjabi or Hausa. This choice of label suggests they have come to the conclusion that most teachers have never heard of – and have little interest in – the languages they speak. Yet it is critical that teachers recognize and respect the skills and experiences which children bring with them.

Language surveys

An important starting point is establishing which languages and dialects are spoken in the school (Nicholas 1994). This can be approached in several ways. Language surveys are now commonplace in many schools, helping to establish not only the range of languages and dialects spoken but the circumstances in which they are used.

A language questionnaire from Redfern 1994

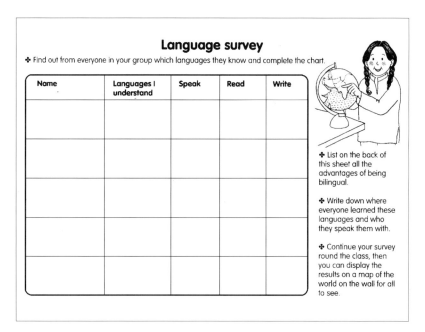

Language surveys can involve the children in questionnaire design and interviews; the analysis and reporting of results also make demands on their mathematical abilities. Most important, though, they are very effective tools for raising awareness of linguistic diversity among both pupils and teachers.

Language gazetteers

Language gazetteers also provide information on linguistic diversity. Some schools have compiled and regularly update booklets which describe the different language backgrounds, writing systems and religions of their children (Katzner, 1986 and Garson et al, 1989 are good reference books on world languages). This information is invaluable when a child arrives speaking a language not previously represented in the school. It is also helpful as part of the induction process for new members of staff.

Country: Ghana

Main language(s): The official language is English. The most important indigenous language is Twi. Other languages include Fanti, Ewe, Ga, Adangme and Dagomba.

Main religion(s): About half the population follow traditional beliefs; 40% Christian; 10% Moslem.

Naming system:
* In some parts of Ghana, children are named after the day of the week they were born, e.g. Akwasi for a boy and Akosua for a girl born on Sunday.
* Piesie is a first child, Manu and Maanu the second consecutive boy and girl; Attaa and Atta girl and boy twins.

Writing: Latin alphabet with some additional letters, e.g. Twi:

> Nantwí bí redidí wɔ sáre bí sò.
> Saá sáre ɏi bèŋ atɛkyé bí â mpɔ̀torɔ áhyɛ́ m̀u mä hɔ̃.
> Mpɔ̀torɔ nó húù ńo ńo, wɔɏ́ mù bínom teɛ́ɛm sè: „Akoá ɏi sò mà nè hɔ́ baá nò.“

Other comments: Education free and compulsory but class sizes are very large.

Naming practices

Many language gazetteers give information on naming practices. Names are very important. Teachers have a responsibility to pronounce them as accurately as possible and to understand that, in different societies, naming practices can be very different. For instance, in most Moslem families, each member has a different last name. Males are given a personal name which is used only by the family and close friends, and a religious name normally used together with the personal name. Sometimes the personal name comes first, sometimes the religious name. Acquaintances will normally use the 'calling name' which consists of the religious and personal name. Some men also have hereditary names which they use as family names.

Moslem men's names

Religious name, eg *Mohammed*

Personal name used by family and close friends, eg *Khalid*

Calling name used by acquaintances, eg *Mohammed Khalid*

Hereditary name sometimes used as family name, eg *Quereshi*

Moslem women's names

First name, eg *Fatma*

Female title, eg *Bibi*

Husband's last name, eg *Aslam*

Formal name, eg *Fatma Bibi* or *Fatma Bibi Aslam* (but not *Mrs Fatma Bibi* which is roughly equivalent to *Mrs Fatma Mrs*)

Moslem women, in contrast, are given first and second names. The first name is personal; the second is either a female title or a second personal name. The second name can act as the family name or, alternatively, the husband's last name is adopted on marriage. Moslems sometimes take on the naming practices in their new country, so there may be still further variations.

Naming practices are thus complex and vary enormously. Teachers may not understand all the many nuances but they cannot assume that Anglo-Saxon conventions apply. They also have a responsibility to ask parents how they and their children should be addressed.

Cross-cultural communication

Teachers also need to understand the nature of cross-cultural differences and how these can sometimes lead to breakdowns in communication. Differences in accent and intonation, for instance, can give rise to serious misunderstanding. One often cited example is the way that Indians and Pakistanis ask questions with a falling rather than a rising intonation which may sound rude or uninterested to British ears. They also tend to lower their voices before making the main point, placing emphasis on the previous sentence. As a result, British speakers often cut in too soon and they, in turn, seem rude.

Our expectations about appropriate behaviour in conversation are largely unconscious. It is only when we come into contact with people whose own experience is different that the seams begin to show. Often we become aware of a rule only when someone breaks it. Take, for example, the question of when it is appropriate to talk. At one end of the spectrum, certain native American groups can wait several minutes before taking a turn in the conversation; at the other end of the spectrum, it is perfectly acceptable in African Caribbean conversations for several people to speak at the same time.

Differences of this kind can cause a great deal of misunderstanding. Robinson (1985) reports a conversation between an American and a Vietnamese student. The American continually asks questions to keep the conversation going, while the Vietnamese usually answers with yes, no or a very short answer. When interviewed later, the American student said she felt the Vietnamese student wasn't interested in her because she never asked any questions in return. The Vietnamese student, in turn, said she felt she didn't have enough time to answer because the American kept firing questions.

There are differences, too, in what people talk about. Certain subjects are legitimate discussion points in some societies but totally taboo in others. In many societies, it is not acceptable, for instance, to talk about childbirth or bodily functions. It is very important for teachers to be sensitive about what can and cannot be discussed and for children to be encouraged to share what they want to share, rather than what the teacher demands.

Respect is another issue which is treated very differently. In many cultures, respect for the teacher is extremely important. This may pose problems in a school system where students challenge and debate, and where teachers expect to be interrupted if students don't understand.

Finally, there are important differences in discourse style, or how we approach a subject. In some societies, you are expected to get 'straight to the point'; in others you have to approach the subject more indirectly. The stories of many African Caribbeans and African Americans, for instance, have no obvious beginning or ending and go on as long as the audience is prepared to listen. Geneva Smitherman (1977: 147–8), an African American linguist, describes this phenomenon in terms of a meandering away from the point which

> takes the listener on episodic journeys and over tributary rhetorical routes, but like the flow of nature's rivers and streams, it all eventually leads back to the source. Though highly applauded by blacks, this narrative linguistic style is exasperating to whites who wish you'd be direct and hurry up and get to the point.

This difference in style has far reaching implications for educators. American research (Michaels 1981; Michaels & Cazden 1986) has focussed on 'sharing time' or 'show and tell', the classroom activity where children report something that has happened to them or talk about something they have brought from home. They are encouraged to be explicit and not to assume that other members of the class will know what they are talking about. Sharing time provides a valuable oral preparation for literacy: it promotes skills such as finding the most important idea, ordering events, and summarizing the main point of a story.

It would seem that Black and White children approach sharing time in different ways. White children tend to have a marked beginning, middle and end to their stories, with no shifts in time and place. They use the same 'topic-centred style' as the teacher, who picks up on what they say and expands it with comments and questions.

In contrast, many Black children have a 'topic associating style'. They tend to tell stories made up of a series of personal anecdotes which shift in time and place and have no explicit point. Teachers sometimes feel that Black children 'ramble on' and interrupt them with inappropriate questions. Yet closer analysis shows that Black children *do* produce well structured stories. They mark topic changes by elongating the vowels of key words and use exaggerated emphasis to show that they are building up to the climax of their story. The problem, then, would seem to lie not in children's ability to structure a story but in teachers' ability to recognize what they are doing.

The implications of these and other differences in discourse style are clear. Teachers need to understand that their own approach to communication is just one among many, and that other groups behave in different ways. They need to be aware of the range of verbal and non-verbal behaviours and the different meanings which these may hold for different cultural groups; and they have a responsibility for discussing these differences with the children that they teach. Equally important, they need to ensure that the prejudices and stereotypes of mainstream White society are not allowed to disadvantage children from ethnic minority communities.

Learning a second language

For many years, new arrivals were placed in special language centres where they were given intensive English language teaching. Over a period of time, there was mounting concern over 'withdrawal' classes where the only English speaking model was the teacher and there was no opportunity to interact with fluent speakers of English. In contrast, the mainstream classroom provided ample opportunities for real communication. There was also a growing appreciation of ways in which maths, science and other areas of the curriculum could support and even increase the potential for language learning. The prevailing wisdom today is that the needs of bilingual learners are best met in mainstream classrooms.

If the logical place for bilingual children is the mainstream classroom, then subject and class teachers must take responsibility for their learning. In many cases, they will be able to call upon the expertise of specialist language support teachers. Support teachers, however, should work in partnership with mainstream teachers, not in isolation.

All teachers in multilingual classrooms need a basic understanding of the language learning process. If children are to learn another language, they need to make sense of what is being said. As fluent speakers of one language, they can draw on their existing knowledge. They know, for instance, what people are likely to say in different situations – greetings, requests, reprimands. They also have a clear idea of how language works and make use of skills such as pattern recognition, generalization and inference to work out the units of the language and how these are built into larger structures.

The speed of language learning depends on a host of variables. The frequency of contact between learners and speakers of English is very important: children learn more quickly when they can interact with lots of English speakers than when all or most of their classmates are language learners. Similarly, when children are expected to work on an individual basis, their opportunities to hear and use the language are very limited. In classrooms organized around group activities, however, their exposure to the language is much greater.

In the very early stages, some children spend several months observing others, but saying little or nothing themselves. This silent period allows children to gain the proficiency and confidence they need to start communicating with native speakers. There is, however, considerable variation between learners. Even when children have the same motivation and opportunities for learning, some take up to five years longer to become proficient English speakers (Wong Fillmore 1991).

It is also important to be aware of different kinds of language proficiency. Most children acquire conversational skills in under two years. In contrast, it takes between five and seven years for second language learners to reach the same levels of proficiency in academic English as their native speaking peers (Cummins 1994). It is not difficult to understand why this should be the case. While conversation is supported by gestures, intonation and other cues to meaning, academic language contains a great deal less contextual support. An obvious implication is that bilingual children continue needing support even after they have achieved conversational fluency.

Supporting language learners

Teachers in multilingual classrooms need to know about the background of bilingual learners. But what about the things that teachers need to do? Which aspects of classroom management and which activities work best in situations where children are at different levels of competence in English?

Providing a secure environment

The enormous emotional strain of arriving in a school unable to speak the language should never be underestimated, whatever the age of the child. Angela Redfern describes the experience of a five year old who had arrived in her class straight from a village in Azad Kashmir

> He had been dressed in a suit and socks and shoes to which he was naturally unaccustomed. He was looked after with concern by fellow speakers of Mirpuri Punjabi in the class. Even so he was none too happy. By the afternoon, tears of misery were running down his cheeks. I had asked the Punjabi speakers in the class to translate everything I thought might help; I had run the gamut of smiles and gestures. There was nothing else I could think of except to clutch him to my bosom and rock him to and fro. One thoughtful child turned the pages of the book for me at story time as I whispered the story so as not to wake the now sleeping child. (Edwards & Redfern 1988: 59)

Fatima, some years after her first arrival, is able to speak for herself about the trauma of arriving in an English classroom:

> When I first came to this country … I found it really hard, I felt like crying because everyone speaks English. I'm the only one who speaks Bengali and if I ask them to explain to me they didn't. (Warner 1991: 14)

Before learning can take place, children need to feel secure. The ones who make the best progress are usually risk takers, straining to communicate even when they know relatively little of the target language. Predictably, children feel free to take risks in secure, supportive classrooms, where teachers are sensitive to their linguistic and cultural background and where they receive encouragement for their efforts.

Second language learning is a slow process. Like learning to play a musical instrument, it is not achieved overnight. It is unrealistic to expect children to produce correct forms of spoken English in the early stages. When a child says 'I have thirsty', it is not at all helpful to stop the communicative flow to point out the mistake. It is perfectly acceptable, though, to provide a correct model in your reply: 'Yes, I'm thirsty, too.' Teachers need to respond sensitively, always remembering that children's comprehension far outstrips their production of spoken English.

It is also important to place your confidence in children as language learners. Beginners in English bring their prior knowledge to the learning of English: they will already be skilled at listening and be able to interpret looks and gestures. They know that patterns of meaning are carried in sounds, structures and intonation and will rapidly tune in to differences in English.

However, children should never be forced to contribute; nor should teachers tolerate 'put downs' from other children. Snide remarks are unfortunately all too common. Pushpa Prabhakar and Mary Morrison (1988) report a range of observations on this subject from 14 and 15 year old students in a Bradford secondary school:

> Many English children take the 'mickey' out of the accent of people who have English as a second language.

> Some words that appear in the English language do not appear in their own so when writing or speaking the English language they would miss it out making the sentence sound very stupid to others. There may be a laugh from some of the boys making the boy feel uneasy. When he is in this depressed state he does not wish to continue. They feel left out when they are in school because they cannot speak the second language.

> You can usually tell a person that cannot speak in English by his appearance. He is usually very quiet, hair is combed very neatly and he looks very dull because of all the 'mickey' people take out of him.

Supportive friends

One practical strategy for reducing stress is to find a supportive partner for any new arrival, preferably, though not necessarily, from the same linguistic background, to help initiate them into playground and classroom routines. It is also important to place them in groups with children who are friendly and ready to help. Wherever possible, the groups should include children who speak the same language.

Survival English

For basic survival, children will need to acquire certain vocabulary and structures as rapidly as possible. They will need to recognize and use simple greetings and politeness formulae such as *hello, goodbye, please* and *thank you;* classroom objects such as *table, chair, book, ruler;* and simple commands and routines such as *sit down, come here* and *can I have?* Some language support services provide teachers with glossaries of 'survival English' accompanied by translations into the main languages in local schools .

While it is clearly important to involve beginners in classroom talk, they should never be pressured to respond. Teachers can help by making what they say as simple as possible: not talking at length; responding to feedback, verbal or non-verbal; and using gestures, the example of other members of the class, and pictures or objects as appropriate. It is also useful to recap on what has happened in a lesson and to mark clearly any change in activity.

Using the first language

Children should be encouraged to use their first language with other bilingual children, teachers and adults to express their needs and queries and to support their learning. Given the level of stress in the early stages of language learning, it is essential that they also use their preferred language for chatting and relaxing with their friends.

Older children have additional needs. They are likely to feel more inhibited than younger learners. It is also very important to recognize the knowledge which they bring with them. Helen Savva (1990) reports the case of a fourteen year boy who had recently arrived from Bangladesh. In response to the simple calculations which his teacher had provided, he wrote a complex algebraic equation on the board, expressing his exasperation with, 'In Bangladesh, me!' Children need to be able to use their strongest or preferred language to gain access to the curriculum. In science, for example, they can synthesize their observations of experiments in their preferred language. They can also be encouraged to record the data in their own language in the early stages.

Creating the right ethos

Monolingual teachers are very dependent on the help of bilingual parents, both in helping to assess the strengths and needs of children and in broadening the range of opportunities for using other languages in the classroom. In many schools, however, relations with ethnic minority parents are not good. Teachers often complain that parents don't come to parents' evening or social events at the school, let alone help out in the classroom. Yet, when this question is approached from the parents' perspective, a very different picture emerges (Edwards & Redfern 1988; Kenway 1994).

Sometimes the problems are purely logistic. Shift workers may find it very difficult to come to evening events. By offering both early afternoon and evening appointments on two or three different days, it is often possible to dramatically increase attendance.

Sometimes parents lack confidence in speaking English. In this case, the knowledge that an interpreter will be present can help to overcome this difficulty.

Parents' own experience of school may also contribute to their feelings of discomfort. It can seem strange and intimidating to be invited to a parents' evening or asked to help in the classroom when you expect teachers to assume sole responsibility for your children's education.

Aspects of school organization can also make a difference. In primary schools, there is, of course, ample opportunity for making contact with parents. Easy access to teaching staff is an extremely important first step in making parents feel comfortable. In some schools, the head teacher stands at the main entrance to greet parents and children at the start and end of the day and keeps the first fifteen minutes of the morning free to deal with any urgent problems. Parents can be asked to deliver their children to the classroom instead of leaving them in the playground. This makes it possible for parents and teachers to exchange information about children and for parents to see their children's work.

In all schools, primary and secondary, a visual environment which includes images and artefacts from other cultures and examples of other languages sends the message to both parents and children that the school values diversity. Until parents feel welcome, little progress can be made.

Activities

It is important to think carefully about the range of opportunities which children have both for listening carefully to native speakers and for experimenting with language themselves.

Many classroom activities involve an element of repetition which is very helpful for the language learner: answering the register, listening to stories or tapes of stories with repetition and rhyme; taking turns in games. With younger children, activities such as building and modelling, playing with sand and water, and sorting and classifying provide an excellent stress free environment for listening to and imitating natural language. Various other classroom activities offer similar opportunities for children of all ages.

Storytelling

Storytelling – as opposed to reading stories – is an effective vehicle for learning, well suited to the needs of bilingual pupils. The use of gesture, eye contact and exaggerated intonation make it easy for language learners to guess what is happening, as do repeated events, cumulative patterns and refrains. Jill Bingham, a student teacher, describes the total involvement of a seven year old Pakistani boy with little English in the following terms:

> Shah Nawaz displayed intense concentration in all our story-telling sessions. This was so great that he was soon asking me to reprimand another child who was interrupting the flow by anticipating what was about to happen next. The stories he liked best were all ones where the actions were as important as the words. His favourite episode in *Sleeping Beauty* was when everyone began to wake from their sleep, accompanied by a great deal of arm stretching, yawning and painful grimacing. In *Tom Tit Tot*, he found the episode where the mother sings and spins most entertaining.

Many bilingual children come from cultures where great importance is attached to storytelling and other forms of oral culture. Austen (1992), a teacher and committed storyteller, reports how the group of children that put their hands up when asked if they have stories told to them will usually include all the Asian children the the class. They are willing and eager to share these stories and are often able to do this in more than one language. According to one child, Nandu, 'My Dad tells me lots of stories. If we're sitting one night watching telly and there's nothing on my Dad just tells me any old story.'

Oral retellings

The power of narrative is such that children encouraged to retell stories told by a teacher or listened to on tape can often bring to the surface skills that are normally untapped. Oral retellings can also be supportive of bilingual children's development in English. Mike Hill and Angela Henry (1991), for instance, report how Asid, a shy, self-effacing 11 year old listened to a taped version of Ted Hughes' *The iron man* over a period of several weeks. Some time later, his teacher asked him if he would like to try retelling the story on tape himself:

> A quiet corner of the staffroom was chosen and in one sitting, Asid told his version of the story, rarely pausing for thinking time. It had been three months since he had last heard *The iron man* tape. The story was well and truly 'in the head' and so, too, were all the 'linguistic structures', which we believe the text had taught him ... no adult in school had ever heard him speak with such a wealth of expressive power or dynamic range.

Asid's sister Kishwar responded in a similar way after listening to a version of the story of Savitri and Satyavan told by her teacher some weeks before. In this story, Savitri, a young princess, searches throughout the world for a suitable husband. Against her father's advice, she marries Satyavan, the simple woodcutter of her choice, only to discover that he is doomed to die within a year. Kishwar demonstrated exceptional fluency and dramatic skill in her retelling, particularly in her aggressive representation of the confrontation between father and daughter.

Children clearly have the ability to recreate stories from memory; they are able to dramatize and shift in and out of role. Such oral retellings are an invaluable preparation for children's writing.

Rhythm, rhymes and lullabies

Parents engage unselfconsciously in activities which help their children's development as language users. From the earliest days, they talk to their children about what they are doing or what they have done; they sing and recite nursery rhymes that often haven't seen the light of day since their own parents performed the same services for them. The warmth of the close physical contact between parent and child sets up an enjoyment of the rhythms and rhymes of language that stays for life. This experience is not, of course, limited to the English speaking world. Lullabies and nursery rhymes are universal.

Rhymes and songs which children know already can be recorded and collected into class books; new ones can be added to their repertoire. They encourage phonological awareness, a skill associated with success in learning to read. Repetition, rhythm and rhyme in books are also the features which help change children from emergent to independent readers.

IT and talk

Although computers usually feature in discussions of children's writing, it is worth remembering that talk is often most productive in situations where the focus is on something else. Wordprocessing, simulations and content-free software for drama and role play all offer opportunities for children to share their ideas and opinions, clarify what they mean, and develop the ability to compromise and reach a consensus. The non-threatening and non-judgmental environment offered in talk around the computer can be particularly helpful for any children who lack confidence, including those in the early stages of language learning.

Academic English

Once children are fluent conversationalists, it is easy to forget that they still need support in academic English. By discussing tasks before children start reading and writing, it is often possible to anticipate words, structures and concepts which may cause difficulties. Careful questioning allows the teacher to establish how much children understand and identify where they need extra help.

Promoting other languages

Teachers often feel that their first responsibility is to teach children English and that any time which children spend using other languages detracts from this main aim. This view is extremely short-sighted. It ignores the fact that a sound foundation in the first language increases children's success in learning subsequent languages; and it overlooks the potential for raising the status of bilingual children by allowing them to demonstrate their skills. It also fails to recognize the importance of exposure to other languages in increasing monolingual pupils' knowledge about language.

Bilingual support

In some schools, monolingual teachers can call on bilingual support teachers, instructors or classroom assistants. Bilingual support can take a wide variety of forms. In the early days the focus tended to be on support for individuals, either recently arrived children or children experiencing learning difficulties. Increasingly though, bilingual support is organized through flexible group work and team teaching which avoid marginalizing bilingual children.

Bilingual support teachers are able to make an important contribution to all the classroom activities described below which promote the use of other languages. They can tap into children's existing knowledge in ways which bring their new learning alive. Their effectiveness is widely acknowledged by monolingual teachers. The presence of a bilingual adult can help build up a picture of the experiences and concepts which children bring with them into school. It also has a noticeable effect on the confidence of bilingual children. Clark (1991: A94) reports the comments of a reception class teacher who had recently been supported by a bilingual colleague thus:

> It is my experience, 99 per cent of the time, that children who have appeared shy and withdrawn even when they had some knowledge of English would blossom after some time of working with the bilingual support teacher and speak exuberantly, initially in the mother tongue and later in English.

Multilingualism in practice

Bilingual teachers clearly have an advantage over their monolingual colleagues in promoting linguistic diversity. However, with careful planning, there is no reason why monolingual teachers should not be equally successful in efforts to encourage other languages and dialects. The first step in this process is to recognize the expertise of bilingual children; the next step is to seek the support of bilingual parents and colleagues.

A wide range of everyday classroom activities lend themselves to the use of two – or more – languages.

Bilingual stories

The power of narrative holds children in rapt attention. In the same way that storytelling in English is a very effective learning tool for language learners, bilingual storytelling can broaden the horizons of monolingual English speakers.

Stories can, of course, be read or told. When bilingual teachers use a book, they can read it first in one language, then in the next. Alternatively, they can read each page in both languages. Monolingual teachers working with bilingual colleagues can alternate in similar ways. The second language can be read as it stands, or retold in a style adapted to the particular needs of the audience.

Stories do not, of course, depend on books. Many teachers are committed storytellers. Professional storytellers – in English and in other languages – are also in ever-increasing demand. For mixed audiences, most bilingual storytellers either tell traditional stories in English or switch between English and another language, allowing listeners to use actions, mimes, facial expressions and tone of voice, as well as the interspersed English, to work out the meaning of the other language.

Bilingual drama

Growing numbers of teachers are exploring the possibilities of bilingual drama, using both professional theatre in education groups and the children themselves. By drawing on children's everyday skills as interpreters, it is possible for them to act out their daily multilingual reality in role play, puppetry and drama and, at the same time, to allow their monolingual peers access to their world. Take the scenario where an English speaking child visits the home of a Panjabi speaking friend. The conversation with parents and grandparents is likely to take place in Panjabi, but the bilingual child will offer summaries and explanations in English. The same pattern applies to many other situations, such as visits to the doctor or parents' evenings at school.

Monica Deb, Mary Morrison and Mandy Oates (1991) offer an interesting discussion of the rich learning experiences offered by bilingual drama. 15 to 16 year old students who had listened to a storytelling session on the theme of betrothal, were asked to develop stories based on their own experience:

> Each group approaches the telling of their stories with a different multilingual slant. One pauses every so often to translate from Punjabi to English using 'interpreters'; another group with two monolingual girls uses English throughout; in another group a monolingual student almost steals the show in her grandmother role by using the few Punjabi phrases she has especially learnt, to great effect; the fourth group inventively use four languages to portray a wrangle between prospective in-laws. The opposing grandmothers use Urdu and Punjabi, the bride-to-be is a Bengali speaker, whilst her brother uses English. Their story flows vividly and dramatically, showing the evidence of very careful planning. We follow the story-line engrossed in the fluency, range of expressiveness and gestures of the girls.

The discussion which followed the performances ranged across issues such as speech styles and registers in different languages, intonation, the differences between dialects and languages, standard languages, the difficulties of translation, differences in the hand movements that accompany different languages and much more. The children went on to write a handbook on storytelling, each producing their own section and drawing on topics such as audience involvement, and the use of different languages and props. They also received bookings from local schools for oral storytelling with younger children.

Knowledge about language

A similar excitement emerges from Caroline Conniff's (1992) description of a project with 14 to 16 year old students which set out to promote the various languages spoken by the children and to demonstrate that the presence of bilingual pupils was an asset rather than a problem.

The class of 32 included 12 bilinguals who knew between them a total of ten different languages. Each bilingual student was allocated a group and made responsible for teaching them to count from one to 20, to conduct a simple conversation and recite a rhyme in the target language.

Later in the project, students were asked to reflect on differences in word order and grammar between English and the target language. The resulting discussion showed children's understanding of how sound systems, grammar and writing systems vary from one language to another; it also helped to raise the status of the bilingual pupils.

One monolingual boy who had initially shown no interest in the project, was won over when he saw a relatively new arrival in the class consulting a Malayalam dictionary. In his written assignment he commented:

> No one had a bad word to say about their teacher nor the language they had learned. Normally foreign people from India, France and Pakistan stay quiet but through this they have been helped to take control of the situation which I think is great. I would like to thank my teacher, who taught me my language, Basheer.

Group work and discussion

Group work has enormous potential for developing speaking and listening skills, although teachers attempting to promote classroom talk have discovered some unexpected problems along the way. One very pressing issue is the different ways that boys and girls behave in groups. Although there are obviously many exceptions to the general trend, boys tend to talk more than girls in mixed groups, they interrupt more and they are often more aggressive. Girls, on the other hand, tend to defer to other people's ideas and offer encouragement and support for other speakers in the group. Even teachers who are aware of these patterns find it difficult to pay equal amounts of attention to boys and girls.

All sorts of strategies have been developed to make sure that girls have equal chances. It is important, for instance, that children have a chance to talk about what is going on and to be involved in making sure that every one has the chance to express themselves. Girls usually find small group work more comfortable than whole class discussion; it can also be helpful to organize all girl and all boy groups for at least some of the time.

Similarly, a range of issues, such as family life or moral values, are best discussed in cultural groups where children and young people share the bonds of similar experiences. If the aim of discussion is to allow children to explore ideas and feelings, it is only natural that they should use the language associated with these experiences. Children are likely to code-switch between English and the language of the home, depending on the situation and the other speakers.

Audiocassettes

The most important resources for developing speaking and listening skills are clearly people who speak other languages. However, the use of audio material also deserves attention (Routh 1994; Multilingual Resources for Children Project 1995).

Several publishers produce tape and story packs: dual language story books accompanied by a tape which uses one side for the English reading and the other for a second language version. Commercially produced tapes can be usefully supplemented by tapes produced in schools by parents, children and bilingual members of staff.

Audiocassettes offer children and parents a range of creative possibilities: telling or reading their own stories on to tape; acting out dialogues and dramas; performing songs, lullabies and rhymes. Effective use, however, depends on providing a comfortable and well organized listening corner: tapes need to be clearly labelled, and catalogued and stored so that children can find them without difficulty.

Interviews

Interviews and surveys offer many opportunities for using other languages. For instance, bilingual children conducting language surveys or collecting information on matters of local interest or conducting interviews for a class newspaper, can choose which language they prefer for drafting and asking questions of other bilinguals.

This is an area in which newly arrived children may be able to make a very useful contribution. As well as carrying out the interviews, they can also help transcribe taperecorded speech if they are literate in the community language. Well established bilingual learners can play a key role in translating what has been said for monolingual members of the class.

Assessment

The assessment of bilingual children's speaking and listening skills is a very complex matter. An accurate picture can only be built up by observing children in a wide range of contexts: in different social groups, in structured and unstructured activities.

Some children find it very stressful to talk to adults, especially in English. Jean Mills (1993: 62) gives the example of seven year old Nazma who never spoke in the presence of a teacher in school and would read her book in English to a friend in a whisper, but could be observed chatting happily at breaktime. She also comments on how five year old Ranjit would often refuse to communicate in a one to one situation but would often talk in English to herself. On one occasion, she gave a running commentary, while totally engrossed in a sorting activity:

> Circle, circle ... Each, Peach , Pear, Plum ... I don't know what you're writing (balances a ring on her head) ... Look, don't fall down ... I'm gonna have the orange ... (makes a pattern of rings) ... two eyes, one nose, a snowman ... It's nearly snowing.

Evidence also needs to be collected over a period of time. Language learning is a slow and ongoing process and it is very easy to overlook children's very real achievements. Some teachers find it helpful to record progress in the early months using a ticklist which charts major landmarks.

Type of behaviour	Month of observation				
	Sept	Oct	Nov	Dec	Jan
Social behaviour					
■ Mixes with pupil(s) who share the same language or culture					
■ Mixes with pupil(s) who do not share the same language/culture					
■ Joins in with playground activities					
■ Interacts when lining up for lessons, lunch etc					
■ Has a friend					
■ Has several friends					
■ Joins in games and practical lessons					
Non-verbal behaviour					
■ Smiles					
■ Gestures					
■ Point					

Other teachers feel unhappy about fitting children into a fixed structure and prefer the greater freedom offered by observation diaries (see, for instance, Barrs *et al* 1988). Entries usually record the social context (eg small group, adult and child, large group) and the learning context (eg play, drama, collaborative reading and writing activities, science, maths) for the speaking or listening activity observed.

Extract from an observation diary

Dec 7th	Is still very shy with me and the other English speaking members of the class, but chats happily to the Panjabi speakers. Mrs Rafiq is always the first port of call when there's a problem. Listens very attentively at story time.
Jan 12th	Became very agitated today when we were doing experiments on electric circuits. He spoke to Fozia in Panjabi, clearly asking for words in English, then announced, 'My brother do that'. First comment he's volunteered in English.

The assessment of bilingual children's skills in all areas of the curriculum is in fact a controversial issue. For instance, it is common for teachers to use tests standardized on monolingual populations which place bilingual learners at a disadvantage (Cummins 1984). Many teachers in England and Wales have expressed concern that any reference to the needs of bilingual learners in the national curriculum has been added as an afterthought with serious implications for how well children perform in formal assessment. Testing arrangements for the revised national curriculum are not at all clear at the time of writing and this is an area which will need careful monitoring.

Stages of development

Many teachers and Local Education Authorities (LEAs) find it useful to discuss bilingual development in different stages. Hounslow LEA (Wolf & Vasquez 1991), for instance, offers the following descriptions of the speaking and listening characteristics of language learners:

- *Beginner*
  Speaks no English, or only a few isolated words learnt prior to arrival. May be silent or may show signs of listening and copying sounds/words.

- *Stage 1*
  Is beginning to identify and remember words and is putting these together into phrases (eg *no come here*) and is using them socially. Still relies heavily on non-verbal gestures. May continue to be silent. Is beginning to understand simple instructions, relying heavily on visual clues.

- *Stage 2*

  Has sufficient English to take part in peer group discussions but is unable to express more complex ideas or sustain a narrative. Is beginning to sort out small grammatical details (eg *he/she*) and is gaining increasing control of the English tense system. At this stage is more interested in communicating meaning than in 'correctness'. Follows most peer group talk and understands most instructions involved in contextualized classroom tasks. May have difficulty in following a sequence of instructions.

- *Stage 3*

  Is confident in English in most situations appropriate to his/her age, but may need help in taking on other registers (eg science investigations). Has a growing command of more complex verbal meanings (eg expressing tentativeness: *might, could* etc). Listens with understanding in most classroom situations but may have difficulty in subjects such as history where information may be decontextualized.

By allocating broad descriptors of this kind to different stages of language learning, we risk creating the impression that development is a series of well defined transitions rather than a gradual progression. However, there are various advantages in talking in this way. It reminds us that language learning is a lengthy and ongoing process; it also provides us with a useful shorthand which keys us in to children's likely levels of competence in English.

First language assessment

Children's progress in English is, of course, just one aspect of their language development. To build up as full as possible a picture of children as language users we also need to know about the range of languages which children use at school and in the community. Schools which use the *Primary language record* (Barrs *et al* 1988) or a similar system of record keeping will consult with several people, including bilingual support teachers. Parents are an invaluable source of information; so, too, are the children themselves.

Information about children's competence in other languages is valuable on a number of different fronts. It provides a useful opportunity to get to know parents and express an interest in the languages and cultures of the home. It can also help in the early detection of learning difficulties. Very often slow progress in school is attributed to the fact that children are learning another language; unfortunately, genuine learning difficulties are sometimes detected very late. By establishing whether parents have concerns – for instance, if one of their children is clearly not progressing as rapidly as the others – it is possible to home in on any problems as speedily as possible.

References

Alladina, S. & Edwards, V. (1991) *Multilingualism in the British Isles.* 2 vols. London: Longman.

Association of Teachers to Pupils from Overseas (ATEPO)(Birmingham Branch)(1970) *Work group on West Indians Report.* Birmingham: ATEPO.

Austen, S. (1992) Storytelling and culture. *Talk* 5: 10–11.

Barrs, M., Ellis, S., Hester, H. & Thomas, A. (1988) *The primary language record.* London: Centre for Language in Primary Education.

Bernstein, B. (1973) *Class, codes and control,* vol. 1. London: Routledge & Kegan Paul.

Bruner, J. (1986) *Actual minds, possible worlds.* Cambridge, Mass: Harvard University Press.

Clark, R. (1991) A community languages project. In Open University (1991), pp. A91–4.

Conniff, C. (1992) Knowledge about language in a multilingual classroom. *The English and Media Magazine* Autumn: 42–5.

Cummins, J. (1984) *Bilingualism and special education: issues in pedagogy and assessment.* Clevedon, Avon: Multilingual Matters.

Cummins, J. (1994) The acquisition of English as a second language. In K. Sprangenberg-Urbschat & R. Pritchard (eds) *Kids come in all languages: reading instruction for ESL students.* New Delaware: International Reading Association, pp. 36–62.

Cummins, J. & Danesi, M. (1990) *Heritage languages: the development and denial of Canada's linguistic resources.* Toronto: Our schools/Our Selves Education Foundation and Garamond Press.

Deb, M., Morrison, M. & Oates, M. (1991) It's so much better when we all work together. Case study 3.17. In Open University (1991), pp. A199–204.

Department of Education and Science (DES)(1971) *The education of immigrants.* London: HMSO.

Edwards, J. (1989) *Language and disadvantage* (2nd edn). London: Cole & Whurr.

Edwards, V. (1979) *The West Indian language issue in British schools.* London: Routledge & Kegan Paul.

Edwards, V. (1983) *Language in multicultural classrooms.* London: Batsford.

Edwards, V. & Redfern, A. (1988) *At home in school: parent participation in primary education.* London: Routledge.

Garson, S., Heilbronn, R. Hill, B. Pomphrey, C. Valentine, A. & Willis, J. (1989) *World languages project.* Sevenoaks, Kent: Hodder & Stoughton.

Graddol, D. & Swann. J. (1988) Trapping linguists: an analysis of linguists' responses to John Honey's pamphlet, 'The language trap'. *Language and Education* 2(2): 95–111.

Hill, M. & Henry, A. (1991) Powerful stories. Case study 3.18. In Open University (1991), pp. A205–9.

Katzner, K. (1986) *The languages of the world.* London: Routledge & Kegan Paul.

Kenway, P. (1994) *Working with parents.* Reading: Reading and Language Information Centre, University of Reading.

Labov, W. (1973) The logic of non-standard English. In N. Keddie (ed)(1973) *Tinker, tailor … the myth of cultural deprivation.* Harmondsworth: Penguin, pp.21–66.

Linguistic Minorities Project (LMP)(1985) *The other languages of England.* London: Routledge.

Michaels, S. (1981) 'Sharing time': children's narrative style and the acquisition of literacy. *Language in Society* 10: 423–42.

Michaels, S. & Cazden, C. (1986) Teacher-child collaboration as oral preparation for literacy. In B. Scheifflin & P. Gilmore (eds.) *The acquisition of literacy: ethnographic perspectives.* Norwood, NJ: Ablex, pp. 132–54.

Mills, J. (1992) Monolingual teachers assessing bilingual children. In R. Mills & J. Mills (eds) *Bilingualism in the primary school.* London: Routledge, pp. 59–72.

Multilingual Resources for Children Project (1995) *Building bridges: multilingual resources for children.* Clevedon: Avon: Multilingual Matters.

National Association of Schoolmasters (NAS) (1969) *Education and the Immigrants.* Hemel Hempstead, Herts: Educare.

Newbolt, H. (1921) *The teaching of English in England.* London: HMSO.

Nicholas, J. (1994) *Language diversity surveys as agents of change.* Clevedon, Avon: Multilingual Matters.

Open University (1991) *Talk and learning 5–16: an inservice pack on oracy for teachers.* Milton Keynes: Open University Press.

Peal, E. & Lambert, W. (1962) The relation of bilingualism to intelligence. *Psychological Monographs* 76: 546.

Prabhakar, P. & Morrison, M. (1988) Being multilingual in secondary school: students raise their own issues. *Oracy issues* 1: 22–3.

Redfern, A. (1994) *Spelling and language skills.* Leamington Spa: Scholastic.

Robinson, G. (1985) *Crosscultural understanding: processes and approaches for foreign language, English as a second language and bilingual educators.* New York: Pergamon.

Routh, C. (1994) *See hear! a guide to audiovisual resources in the primary school.* Reading: Reading and Language Information Centre, University of Reading.

Savva, H. (1990) The rights of bilingual children. In R. Carter (ed.) (1990) *Knowledge about language and the curriculum.* Seven Oaks, Kent: Hodder & Stoughton, pp. 248–68.

Smitherman, G. (1977) *Talkin' and testifyin': the language of Black America.* Boston: Houghton Mifflin.

Tizard, B. & Hughes, M. (1984) *Young children learning.* London: Fontana.

Vygotsky (1978) *Mind in society: the development of higher psychological processes.* Cambridge, Mass: Harvard University Press.

Warner, R. (1991) Bangladesh is my motherland. *The English and Media Magazine* Summer: 12–15.

Wolf, A. & Vasquez, M. (1991) *Teaching beginners in secondary schools.* Hounslow: Hounslow Language Service.

Wong Fillmore, L. (1991) Second language learning in children: a model of language learning in social context. In E. Bialystok (ed.) *Language processing in bilingual children.* Cambridge: Cambridge University Press, pp. 49–69.

Wood, D., McMahon, L. & Craunston, Y. (1980) *Working with under fives.* London: Grant Mc.